Published by Blackbirch Press, Inc.
260 Amity Road
Woodbridge, CT 06525

web site: http://www.blackbirch.com
e-mail: staff@blackbirch.com

©1998 Blackbirch Press, Inc.
First Edition

Printed in the United States of America

10 9 8 7 6 5 4 3 2 1

Index Compiled by: Elizabeth Kniss

Index Editor: Laura P. Norton

Library of Congress Cataloging-in-Publication Data

Holocaust : cumulative index for volumes 1 to 8. — 1st ed.
     p.   cm.
    Summary: Illustrated with photographs, this volume indexes the first eight volumes of the series.
    ISBN 1-56711-209-9 (library binding : alk. paper) ISBN 1-56711-212-9 (pbk.)
    I. Holocaust (Woodbridge, Conn.)—Indexes. 2. Holocaust, Jewish (1939–1945)—
Juvenile literature—Indexes. [1. Holocaust (Woodbridge, Conn.)—Indexes. 2. Holocaust, Jewish (1939–1945)—Indexes.]
D804.34.H65 1998
940.53'18—dc21   97-25619
                                                                 CIP
                                                                  AC

Cumulative
Index

Volumes 1 through 8

A   B L A C K B I R C H   P R E S S   B O O K

W O O D B R I D G E ,   C O N N E C T I C U T

A

Abella, Irving, 8:27

Abraham, "father of Judaism," 1:**14**–16

Abrahamson, Samuel, 8:12

Abzug, Robert H., 8:31

Albritten, David, 2:38

Alexander, Ellen, 7:**27**–28

Alexander II, Czar of Russia, 1:39

Alexander the Great, 1:17

Ali, Rashid, 3:26

Allen, William S., 8:15

Allied forces, 5:44–46, **45**, 63; 7:67

Altshuler, David A., 8:10

Altusky, Hirsh, 3:46; 4:56

Abraham and Isaac

Amsterdam, 8:15, 57, 67

See also Holland

"Angel of Death." *See* Mengele, Josef

Anielewicz, Mordecai, 4:67–69, **68**; 7:59

Anschluss, 2:51–52, 54; 3:13; 4:55; 7:19–**21**

Antisemitism

in Austria, 4:55

at Berlin Olympics, 2:36, 38

conspiracy theories about Jews, 1:48

description and history of, 1:11–12, 22; 3:11–12; 4:21

during early modern era (1500s–1600s), 1:36–37

in France in the 1800s, 1:42–44

in Germany in the 1800s, 1:41

goals of Nazi Party, 3:39, 42, 67; 4:10–11; 5:10; 7:8, 31–32, 45, 51

growth of in Hitler, 1:54

in Italy, 2:41–44

during Middle Ages, 1:26–28, 30–33

passing of Nuremberg Laws, 2:20, 22; 7:17–19

in Poland, 2:33; 4:60–61; 7:18–19

reference books about, 8:7, 9–11, 13–14, 16, 18, 37–38

in schools, 1:38, 67

in United States, 2:32

videos about, 8:48, 59

Austrians welcome Hitler after the *Anschluss*, 1938.

web sites about, *8*:67–69

after World War II, *6*:22, 34

See also Hitler, Adolf; homosexuals; Jehovah's
Witnesses; mentally dis-
abled; Nazi Party; Nazis;
non-Jews; Romani

Arab reaction to Jews, *6*:36–37,
39–40, 42

Arad, Yitzhak, *8*:18, 28

Artz, Louis, *5*:10

"Aryan" race
in Berlin Olympics, *2*:35, 37

"cleansing," *7*:33

control over German
economy, *2*:44–45

Hitler's acquisition of Poland
for living space, *4*:60

Hitler's theories about, *1*:56;
2:20; *7*:8

laws supporting, *1*:65

Ashkenazi Jews, *1*:23, 39

Athletes, Jewish, *2*:36–37, 39

Atomic bomb, *2*:44; *3*:27

Auerbacher, Inge, *3*:24–26, 68;
8:32

Auschwitz–Birkenau concentration camp, 5:**52**
  as city before World War II, 3:32
  death marches from, 5:57, 60–61; 6:10–11
  descriptions of deportations to, 7:46–47, 63–64
  descriptions of life in, 7:53–57, 65–66
  evacuation of, 5:60–61
  gassing of Jews at, 4:30, 51; 5:49, 54–55, 58
  illustrated books about, 8:41
  liberation of, 5:60–61; 6:11
  mass murders at, 4:48
  overview of, 4:29–30; 5:18–19
  reference books about, 8:20–21, 32, 34–37
  revolt at, 5:55–56
  tattooing in, 4:43–44
  testing of Zyklon B gas, 3:68
  videos about, 8:51, 53, 59, 62–63
  web sites about, 8:66–67
Austria
  annexation of, 2:51–52, 54; 3:13; 4:55; 7:19–**21**
  antisemitism in, 4:55
  emigration of Jews, 2:58–60
  Nazi violence in, 2:52–55; 3:13
  reference books about, 8:15, 35
Avni, Haim, 8:12
Avriel, Ehud, 2:53

Axis powers, formation of, 3:59
Ayer, Eleanor H., 8:12, 36

B

Bach, H. I., 8:8
Bachrach, Susan D., 8:10
Baeck, Leo and Samuel, 2:26
Balfour Declaration of 1917, 3:23; 6:36–37
Banks, Lynn Reid, 6:43
Barbie, Klaus, 6:**49**–51
Bauer, Yehuda, 6:72; 8:10, 36
Bavaria, Hitler's march on, 1:55
Beck, Ludwig, 3:18
Becker, Dr., 4:20
Belgium
  German invasion of, 2:49; 3:53
  protection of Jews in, 4:46
  videos about, 8:47, 55

Klaus Barbie

The Bielski partisans, in a forest in Poland.

Belzec death camp, 4:27–28, 52; 5:19
Benes, Eduard, 2:60; 3:19
Ben-Gershom, Ezra, 6:33
Ben-Gurion, David, 6:**41**, 48
Benites, Manuel, 3:24
Berben, Paul, 8:20
Berenbaum, Michael
  description of Nazi confisca-tion of Jewish belongings, 4:54
  description of Raoul

Wallenberg, 5:59
description of United States Holocaust Memorial Museum, 6:71
edited reference books by, 8:6, 21, 30, 39
reference books by, 8:11
view of Holocaust, 1:13
Berg, Mary, 4:36, 38
Bergen-Belsen concentration camp, 4:45; 5:68–70; 6:14, 21

Brown-shirts burn the Weimar flag on the streets of Berlin, 1933.

Berger, David, 8:37
Berger, Stephen, 7:**62**–64
Bergmann, Gretel, 2:36–37
Berlin
   destruction of synagogues,
     2:62, 67
   Olympics, 2:**34**, 35–**39**; 8:48
   reference books about, 8:12
Bernstein, Cecilia, 2:32; 5:27–28
Bethune, Mary McLeod, 2:23
Bialystok ghetto
   revolt, 5:17
   video about, 8:54
Bielski, Tuvia, 5:47–48

Bielski partisans, 4:21–**22**;
   5:47–48; 8:24
   See also resistance groups
Birkenau death camp. *See*
   Auschwitz–Birkenau concentration camp
Bismarck, Prince Otto von,
   1:51
"Black Death," 1:29–31, 30
Black-shirts, 1:**58**
   attack on Warsaw ghetto,
     4:69–72; 7:58–59
   control over Hungary, 5:36
   death marches, 6:15

description of abuses by, *2*:54, 69

Einsatzgruppen, *4*:**8**, **17**
   establishment of, *3*:41–42
   mass murders by, *1*:43; *3*:64–67; *4*:9
   orders from Reinhard Heydrich, *7*:31
   role of, *4*:16–18
   use of gassing vans, *3*:64–65; *4*:**20**, 46–47; *5*:19

evacuation of concentration camps, *6*:15

overthrowing of at Auschwitz–Birkenau, *5*:56

resistance against, *4*:28–29, 65

role of, *2*:25; *3*:41–42, 64–67; *4*:10, 16–18; *5*:10

sheltering of after World War II, *6*:45

union with Gestapo, *2*:51

at Wannsee Conference, *4*:19

war crimes, *6*:25–31; *7*:73

See also Gestapo

Blatt, Tomasz, *5*:25–26

Blatter, Jane, *8*:40

Blobel, Paul, *4*:18

Block, Gay, *8*:24

Blood libel, *1*:26–28, **27**

"Bloody Thursday," *4*:27

Bogen, Alexander, *8*:40

Book-burnings, *1*:65, **66**; *7*:31

Borchmeyer, Erich, *2*:38

Bormann, Martin, *6*:27, 31, 46

Bourke-White, Margaret, *5*:44, 66

Bower, Tom, *6*:49

Boyarin, Jonathan, *8*:9

Boycott of Jewish shops, *1*:63, **64**, 65; *7*:**9**–10, 17, 19

Braham, Randolph L., *8*:13

Braun, Eva, *5*:72

Browning, Christopher, *8*:28

Brown-shirts, *2*:16, 65; *3*:11; *7*:10

Brundage, Avery, *2*:38

Brunner, Alois, *6*:46

Bubonic plague, *1*:29–31

Buchenwald concentration camp, *4*:**24**, **43**; *5*:**8**, **21**; *8*:**20**
   after *Kristallnacht*, *2*:68
   description of life in, *2*:46
   enlargement of, *2*:61

Hitler at a Nuremberg rally, 1935.

evidence from for
    Nuremberg Trials, 6:28
liberation of, 5:64–66; 6:11,
    15; 7:69
reference books about, 8:21,
    35
videos about, 8:51, 53, 64
Buergenthal, Thomas, 5:60–61
Bulgaria, 4:65; 8:13
Buna-Monowitz labor camp,
    4:29–30; 5:18
Burden of Hitler's Legacy
    (Heck), 6:61
"Butcher of Lyons," 6:49–51
Bystanders, reference books
    about, 8:7, 27–30

C

Canada, 8:27
Carlebach, Emil, 2:69
Carr, William, 8:16
Catherine, Czarina of Russia,
    1:37
CD-Roms, 8:69
Censorship, 2:13
Chamberlain, Neville, 2:60, **61**;
    3:18, 20, 30; 6:**37**
Chary, Frederick B., 8:13
Chasid, Joseph and Rachel, 5:**38**
Chelmno death camp, 4:16, 18,
    27; 5:19, 60; 6:10
Children, 5:**52**
    death counts of, 5:70; 6:19
    deportation of, 4:44
    as first to die, 4:13, 43;
        5:39–41, 49, 54; 7:51

as holocaust survivors,
    6:57–58
illustrated books about,
    8:41–42
Kindertransport, 7:27–28
of the Lodz ghetto, 7:58
memorial at Yad Vashem,
    6:70
overview of Holocaust
    experience, 5:70
reference books about, 8:25,
    27, 32–35, 38
rescue of, 7:41–42
videos about, 8:45, 49,
    55–56, 61–62
of the Warsaw ghetto, 4:**34**,
    36–38, 41; 7:52
web sites about, 8:66
China, Jewish asylum in, 3:22
Christianity
    conversion of Jews, 1:24–26,
        31–32, 39
    history of antisemitism, 1:11,
        22
    split with Judaism, 1:12
    See also religion
Chronology
    of Holocaust 1933–1945, 1:72
    of Jewish History 70
        C.E.–1935, 1:70–71
Churchill, Winston, 3:23, 55–56;
    5:63; 6:26, 36
Cohen, Benno, 2:67
Cohn, Norman, 1:26
Coleman, Hugh, 8:8
Collaborators, 5:**57**; 8:27–30
Communist Party, 2:10, 26

Prisoners at Buchenwald, 1945

Concentration camps
  Auschwitz–Birkenau, *5:***52**
    as city before World War II,
      3:32
    descriptions of deportations
      to, *7:46–47, 63–64*
    descriptions of life in,
      7:53–57, 65–66
    gassing of Jews at, *4:30, 51;*
      5:49, 54–55, 58
    illustrated books about,
      8:41
    liberation of, *5:60–61; 6:11*
    mass murders at, *4:48*
    overview of, *4:29–30;*
      5:18–19

    reference books about,
      8:20–21, 32, 34–37
    revolt at, *5:55–56*
    tattooing in, *4:43–44*
    testing of Zyklon B gas,
      3:68
    videos about, *8:51, 53, 59,*
      62–63
    web sites about, *8:66–67*
  Bergen-Belsen, *4:45; 5:68–70;*
    6:14, 21
  Buchenwald, *4:***24**, **43***; 5:***8**,
    21, *64–66; 6:15–16; 8:***20**
    after *Kristallnacht, 2:68*
    description of life in, *2:46*
    enlargement of, *2:61*

A Nazi collaborator in Belgium is marked with a swastika after liberation, in 1944.

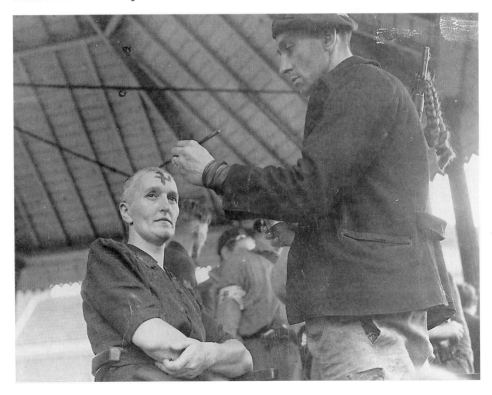

evidence from for
  Nuremberg Trials, 6:28
liberation of, 5:64–66;
  6:11, 15; 7:69
reference books about,
  8:21, 35
videos about, 8:51, 53, 64
Buna-Monowitz, 4:29–30;
  5:18
conditions in, 1:**10**; 4:54–56;
  7:48, 50, 54–57, 64, 66
Dachau, 5:**21**, **68**
  death marches from,
    5:70–71
  description of life in,
    5:70
  establishment of, 1:62
  evidence from for
    Nuremberg Trials, 6:28
  liberation of, 5:**68**, 70–71;
    6:11, 16; 7:69–71; 8:60
  reference books about,
    8:20, 32
  videos about, 8:51, 60–61
  web sites about, 8:67
early operation, 2:26
enlargement of, 2:61
establishment of, 1:62;
  3:12–13; 7:45
in France, 8:51
general description of, 5:66;
  8:20–21, 40, 42
Gurs, 7:37, 39–42
Kaufering, 7:66
Kratzau, 6:17
liberation of, 5:65 (map),
  68; 6:13

Prisoners await gassing at Chelmno, 1942.

Auschwitz-Birkenau,
  5:60–61; 6:11
Bergen-Belsen, 5:69–70;
  6:14
Buchenwald, 5:64–66;
  6:11, 15–16; 7:69
Dachau, 5:**68**, 70–71;
  6:11, 16; 7:69–71; 8:60
Kratzau, 6:17
Mauthausen, 6:14–15
Ohrdruf, 5:63; 6:15–16
Ravensbrück, 5:71–72
reference books about,
  8:31–32
Theresienstadt, 6:16
videos about, 8:60–61

14

Prisoners from Dachau on a forced death march in 1945, just before liberation.

listing/descriptions of
  largest, 5:20–21
locations of, 5:17 (map);
  7:75 (chart)
Mauthausen, 4:**51**, 54;
  6:14–15; 8:53
Ohrdruf, 5:63–64; 6:11,
  15–16
Ravensbrück, 5:71–72
resistance in, 5:55–58;
  8:23
Sachsenhausen, 2:68–69
Strasshoff, 7:63
Theresienstadt, 5:**39**
  description of, 7:49–50
  general overview of, 5:40
  illustrated books about,
    8:41–42

liberation of, 6:16
reference books about,
  8:32, 34
treatment of elderly,
  4:25–26
videos about, 8:52
treatment of prisoners,
  2:45–46, 68–69; 4:25–26;
  5:70; 7:48, 50, 53–57,
  64–66
videos about, 8:60–61
Westerbork transit camp,
  4:**31**; 8:**34**, 50
See also death camps
Conot, Robert E., 8:31
Conversion of Jews, 1:24–26,
  31–32, 39
Costanza, Mary S., 8:40

Country/cultural studies, *8*:8, 11–15
See also foreign reaction to
Cracow ghetto, *3*:**47**; *5*:31
See also ghettos
Craig, Gordon A., *8*:16
Crematoriums, *6*:**29**
deportations to, *7*:48–49, 65–66
description of, *3*:43; *4*:18; *5*:61
establishment of, *4*:27
Crimes, Nazi Party, *6*:25–31; *7*:73
charges against defendants, *6*:26–27
description of defendants, *6*:27–28
hunting of criminals, *6*:46–51
trials and punishments, *6*:29–31
Cromwell, Oliver, *1*:36
Crusades, persecution of Jews during, *1*:24–26, 25
See also Middle Ages (500–1500 C.E.)
"Crystal Night." *See* *Kristallnacht*
Cuban reaction to Jewish refugees, *3*:24–25; *7*:28–29
Cultural traditions, Jewish, *1*:19, 21, 41–43
Czak, Ibola, *2*:38
Czarnecki, Joseph P., *8*:41
Czech, Danuta, *8*:20
Czechoslovakia

deportations in, *3*:26
German invasion of, *2*:49, 60–61; *3*:15, 18–21, 26
increasing violence in, *3*:21
Jewish refugees in, *3*:26
Nazi destruction of Lidice, *4*:33
reference books about, *8*:8–9
videos about, *8*:44, 61–63
Czerniakow, Adam, *4*:36, 38–**39**; *7*:52

D

Dachau concentration camp, *5*:**21**, **68**
description of life in, *5*:70
establishment of, *1*:62
evidence from for Nuremberg Trials, *6*:28
forced death marches from, *5*:70–71
liberation of, *5*:**68**, 70–71; *6*:11, 16; *7*:69–71; *8*:60
reference books about, *8*:20, 32
videos about, *8*:51, 60–61
web sites about, *8*:67
Danish Jews, *5*:**22**, 23
See also Denmark
Dawidowicz, Lucy, *1*:13; *8*:11
D-Day, *5*:44–46; *6*:10
See also allied forces
"Death boxes." *See* ghettos
Death camps
Auschwitz–Birkenau, *5*:**52**

Allied troops land on the beaches of Normandy, France, D-Day 1944.

locations of, *5*:17 (map);
7:75 (chart)
Majdanek, *5*:19, 32; *8*:32
reference books about,
8:20–21
Sobibór, *4*:30–32; *5*:19,
22–23, 25–26
Treblinka, *4*:40; *5*:22
videos about, *8*:50–53, 60
See also concentration
camps
Death counts, Jewish, *1*:10;
5:69 (chart); *6*:16, 19, 21;
7:59, 75 (chart)
Death marches, *5*:**42**, 51
(map); 7:65
from Auschwitz–Birkenau,
5:57, 60–61; *6*:10–11
description of, 7:67, 70
Delbo, Charlotte, *8*:32
Denmark, *8*:24, 27, 58
Deportations, 7:**34**
after allied invasion of
Europe, *5*:46–47, 49, 51
(map)
to Auschwitz–Birkenau concentration camp, 7:46–47,
63–64
to Belzec death camp, *4*:27
of children, 7:51
to crematoriums, 7:48–49,
65–66
of Czechoslovakian Jews,
3:26
definition of, *4*:10
description of, *4*:17–18;
7:38–43, 46–47, 49–50,
53–54
by *Einsatzgruppen*, *4*:16–18
from ghettos, *5*:16–17
goals of Wannsee
Conference, *4*:18–19; 7:45
of Hungarian Jews, *5*:36–37;
7:61–64
increase of, *4*:19–21, 25, 29,
33; *5*:**12**, 16–17 (map);
7:34
of Jews to France, 7:38–43
"Operation Reinhard," *4*:33
of Polish Jews, *3*:34; 7:22–23,
48–49, 51–52

A man awaits deportation in Poland, 1942.

to Sobibór, *4*:30–31
train conditions, *5*:27–28
from Warsaw ghetto,
    4:38–39; *7*:52
Der Judenstaat (Herzl), *6*:35
Des Pres, Terrence, *8*:20
Dessau, Netti Golde, *2*:16
Detention camps, *5*:27
Deutsch, Madeline, *6*:55
Diaries, *8*:6, 18–19, 22, 29,

Antisemitic cartoon about the Dreyfus Affair in an Austrian newspaper.

    31–35, 42, 49
Dimendberg, Edward, *8*:17
Dippel, John V. H., *8*:16
Discrimination. *See* antisemitism;
    Hitler, Adolf; homosexuals;
    Jehovah's Witnesses; mentally
    disabled; Nazi Party; Nazis;
    Romani
Displaced Persons (DPs)
    camps, *6*:20–23
    description of, *7*:71–**72**
Di Umberto, Michele, *3*:59
Dobroszycki, Lucjan, *8*:8, 13, 18
Donat, Alexander, *8*:32
"Dreyfus Affair," *1*:42–44, 48;
    6:35
Drucker, Malka, *8*:24
Drucker, Olga Levy, *8*:32
Dutch Jews, *4*:**43**, 48
    See also Holland
Dwork, Deborah, *8*:20, 38

E

Early modern era (1500s–1600s)
    easing of antisemitism,
        1:36–37
    Judaism during, *1*:35
Eban, Abba, *6*:70
Economic decline of Jews,
    2:16–17, 27, 29–30, 44–45, 71
Edelheit, Abraham J., *8*:6–7
Edelheit, Hershel, *8*:6–7
Edelman, Marek, *4*:70
Eden, Anthony, *2*:33
Education
    antisemitism in, *1*:38, 67
    Nazi influence on, *2*:15,
        23–24, 30–32; *7*:12
    in Warsaw ghetto, *4*:37
Ehrman, Felice, *7*:49–50
Eichmann, Adolf
    as director of emigration in

Czechoslovakia, *3*:21
establishment of *Judenrate*
in Hungary, *5*:36–37
establishment of Office of
Jewish Emigration, *2*:57
evacuation of Jews, *3*:39
genocide planning, *4*:10–11
trial and hanging of,
6:47–48, 56
use of gassing vans, *4*:46
at Wannsee Conference,
4:19
witness to cremations at
Chelmno death camp,
4:16
Eiger, David, *3*:36
Einsatzgruppen, *4*:8, 17
establishment of, *3*:41–42
mass murders by, *1*:43;
3:64–67; *4*:9
orders from Reinhard
Heydrich, *7*:31
role of, *4*:16–18
use of gassing vans,
3:64–65; *4*:**20**, 46–47; *5*:19
Einstein, Albert, *1*:56; *2*:13; *3*:**27**
Eisenhower, Dwight D., *5*:**62**,
63, 66; *6*:11, 16
Eishishok, Lithuania, *1*:42–43
Elderly Jews, treatment of,
4:25–26
Emigrants, Jewish, *1*:65, 67
See also refugees, Jewish
Engelmann, Bernt, *2*:66
Epidemic, typhus, *3*:63–64;
5:68–70; *6*:16
Epstein, Helen, *8*:36

Hotel Royal at Evian

Escape attempts, Jewish,
4:28–29, 47; *7*:49, 61, 70
See also resistance groups
Europe, 1935, *2*:11 (map)
Evian Conference, *2*:**56**, 57;
3:22; *4*:53; *7*:22
Exodus from Europe 1947,
6:42
Experiments, medical, *3*:48;
5:18
Expulsion of Jews
from England and France,
1:28
from Germany, *1*:65; *2*:27,
49, 63–64, 71–72 (graph);
3:17–18; *7*:45, 72
from Spain, *1*:31
Extermination camps. *See*
death camps
Ezergailis, Andrew, *8*:13

F

Fasanenstrasse synagogue, *2*:**62**
Fascism, *1*:56; *2*:42–43
Feig, Konnilyn G., *4*:26, 54;
    5:19, 40; *8*:20
Fein, Helen, *6*:63
Feingold, Henry L., *8*:28
Ferdinand, King of Spain, *1*:31
Ferenwald transit camp, *7*:70
Fermi, Enrico and Laura, *2*:44
Fest, Joachim C., *8*:16
Finland, *8*:14
Fischl, Petr, *5*:40–41
Flag, German, *1*:68
Flam, Gila, *8*:38

Flannery, Edward H., *8*:37
Flatow, Alfred and Gustav, *2*:39
Flender, Harold, *8*:24
Fluek, Toby Knobel, *8*:33, 41
Fogelman, Eva, *8*:24
Foley, Frank, *2*:71
Foreign reaction to
    Hitler's aggression, *3*:20
    Jewish refugees
        after World War II, *6*:23
        in Cuba, *3*:24–25; *7*:28–29
        in Czechoslovakia, *3*:26
        debate in America, *3*:23
        debate in Great Britain,
            3:23–24

The Fasanenstrasse synagogue in Berlin after *Kristallnacht*.

Fasanenstrasse—Foreign reaction

emigration numbers by countries, *2*:58, 72 (chart); *3*:22
at Evian Conference, *2*:56–57; *3*:22; *4*:53; *7*:22
in Palestine, *3*:54; *4*:23
reference books about, *8*:27–28
refusal of admittance by countries, *2*:59; *3*:18, 22; *4*:23; *6*:23; *7*:25, 28–29
on *St. Louis* (ship), *3*:25; *7*:28–29
massacre of Jews, *4*:32; *5*:13; *7*:57
Nazism
at Berlin Olympics, *2*:36–37
boycott of Jewish shops, *1*:63
increase of Nazi support groups in foreign countries, *2*:32
lack of foreign confrontation, *1*:10; *2*:49; *3*:18; *7*:16
Nuremberg Laws, *2*:23
reference books about, *8*:8, 10, 13–15, 27–30, 39
Nazi war crimes, *6*:26
"Forest communities," *4*:21–22
Forest of the Dead, The (Wiechert), *2*:26
Fourth Reich Skinheads, *6*:67

France
antisemitism in, *1*:42–44
deportation of Jews to, *7*:38–43
expulsion of Jews, *1*:28
German invasion of, *3*:56–57
Gurs concentration camp in, *7*:37, 39–42
Le Chambon, *7*:41–43; *8*:25, 59
reference books about, *8*:9, 14–15, 22–23, 25, 29
videos about, *8*:47, 51, 58–59
Franco, Francisco, *2*:41
Frank, Anne, *4*:**57**; *7*:**67**
death of, *4*:45; *7*: 67
deportation from Auschwitz–Birkenau, *5*:57
diary of, *2*:49; *3*:55; *4*:45, 56–57; *5*:53; *7*:67; *8*:33
Nazi torment in Holland, *2*:49; *3*:55
reference books about, *8*:25, 33
train trip to Auschwitz–Birkenau, *5*:53
web sites about, *8*:67
at Westerbork transit camp, *4*:31
Frank, Edith, *3*:55; *4*:45; *5*:57
Frank, Hans, *3*:72; *5*:**16**
Frank, Henry, *2*:21
Frank, Margot, *3*:55
Frank, Otto, *2*:49, 54; *3*:55; *4*:45, 56–57

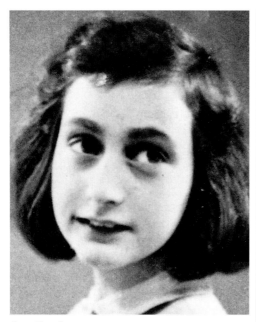

Anne Frank

Freiberg, Ber Moiseyevich, *4*:32

Freidenreich, Harriet Pass, *8*:8

Friedlander, Henry, *8*:30

Friedlander, Saul, *8*:16

Friedman, Ina R., *8*:30

Friedman, Philip, *8*:24

Fuhrer-Ex: Memoirs of a Former Neo-Nazi (Hasselbach), *6*:66

Furnaces, crematory. *See* crematoriums

Furstner, Wolfgang, *2*:39

Furth, Valentine Jacober, *8*:41

G

Gale, Manny, *3*:9–10, 19

Gallagher, Hugh Gregory, *8*:31

Gallant, Rene, *6*:40

Gassing of Jews
  at Auschwitz–Birkenau concentration camp, *4*:30, 51; *5*:49, 54–55, 58
  at Belzec death camp, *4*:27
  at Chelmno death camp, *4*:16
  children, *5*:49, 54–55
  in death camp showers, *3*:43; *5*:22
  description of, *3*:43
  testing of Zyklon B gas, *3*:67–68
  at Treblinka death camp, *4*:40
  in vans, *3*:64–65; *4*:**20**, 46–47; *5*:19

Gebirtig, Mordechai, *4*:47

Gedye, G.E.R., *2*:55

Genocide
  conditions for, *6*:62, 72
  definition of, *1*:9
  modern examples, *6*:61–64
  Nazi Party's plans for, *3*:39, 42, 67; *4*:10–11; *5*:10; *7*:8, 31–32, 45, 51
  videos about, *8*:45–46
  web sites, *8*:69

Genocide Convention, *7*:74

Genocide Watch (Fein), *6*:63

Gentiles. *See* non-Jews

Germany
  allied invasion of Europe, *5*:44–46, 45, 63; *7*:67
  as ally to Italy, *2*:41–42
  antisemitism during the 1800s, *1*:41

aryanization of economy,
2:44–45

cover-up of mass killings,
7:61

current awareness of
Holocaust, 6:69

defeat in World War II,
6:9–11

domination in Europe, 4:14
(map); 5:11 (map)

economic problems after
World War I, 1:51

emigration of Jews, 1:65;
2:27, 49, 63–64, 71–72
(graph); 3:17–18; 7:45, 72

historical overview, 8:15–18,
46–49

Hitler's Reich, 1:51; 3:14
(map); 5:9

Hitler's rise to chancellor,
1:59–60

invasion of
Austria, 2:51–52, 54; 3:13;
4:55; 7:19–21
Belgium, 2:49; 3:53
Czechoslovakia, 2:49,
60–61; 3:15, 18–21, 26
European countries,
2:41–42; 4:9; 5:9
France, 3:56–57
Great Britain, 3:56
Hungary, 5:36
Norway, 3:52–53
Poland, 3:27, 29–32; 4:60;

Hitler greets President von Hindenburg in Berlin, 1934.

7:30–31
Rhineland, *2*:30–31
Soviet Union, *3*:59, 64;
  4:19
Italy declares war on,
  5:26–28
military buildup, *2*:12, 27, 45
public reaction to Nazi atroci-
  ties, *5*:44, 67
public reaction to Nuremberg
  Laws, *7*:18
role in World War I, *1*:50
surrender in World War II,
  5:72
Weimar government, *1*:50–51,
  59; *7*:11; *8*:17
Gestapo
  arrests by, *2*:25; *4*:10
  description of violence by,
    5:15; *7*:22–23
  role of, *2*:14; *3*:39; *5*:10
  union with German police,
    2:51
  See also SS (*Schutzstaffel*)
Ghettos
  Amsterdam, *4*:48
  Bialystok, *5*:17; *8*:54
  conditions in, *3*:62–63, 69–70;
    7:47
  Cracow, *3*:**47**; *5*:31
  definition of, *4*:11
  deportations from, *4*:38–39;
    5:16–17; *7*:52
  establishment of, *1*:37;
    7:32–33, 49
  general overview of, *8*:40, 42
  in Hungary, *7*:62–64; *8*:13

in Lithuania, *8*:23
Lodz, *3*:**45–46, 63**; *4*:**36, 46**;
  7:**36**; *8*:**68**
  children of, *7*:58
  establishment of, *3*:43–**46**;
    7:35
  liquidation of, *5*:49
  reference books about,
    8:18–19, 35, 38
  videos about, *8*:49–50
Lvov, *4*:48
Minsk, *4*:27
Radom, *4*:26; *8*:**39**
Riga, *4*:46; *8*:19
Vilnius, *5*:16; *7*:61; *8*:18, 54
Warsaw, *3*:**40, 49**; *4*:**34**; *7*:**37,
  52**; *8*:**41**
  children of, *4*:**34**, 36–38,
    41; *7*:52
  description of, *3*:44–47;
    4:35–36; *7*:36
  liquidation of, *4*:38–41, 48,
    66, 67–72
  reference books about,
    8:19, 22–24, 32, 34–35
  schools in, *4*:37
  smuggling in, *4*:**37**–38
  uprising in, *4*:68–**72, 71**;
    7:58–59
  videos about, *8*:49–50,
    54–55, 64
Gies, Miep, *2*:54; *8*:25
Gilbert, Martin
  description of "Aryan laws,"
    1:65
  description of Nazi violence,
    5:16, 45, 71

Burial wagon on a Warsaw ghetto street, 1941.

reference books by, *8*:7, 11, 28, 36

Glickman, Marty, *2*:38

God, Jewish view of, *1*:15–16

Goebbels, Josef, *2*:13; *3*:12; *4*:33

Gold, Alison L., *8*:25

Goldmann, Nahum, *2*:42

Gordon, Sarah, *8*:16

Göring, Hermann, *2*:**61**; *6*:**24**, 27, 29, **30**

Gotthold, Helene, *3*:33

Graebe, H.F., *4*:17–18

Graves, mass, *3*:**65**; *4*:**8**
    "Bloody Thursday," *4*:26–27
    description of, *3*:64; *4*:9, 17–18; *5*:16, 60

Great Britain
    control of Palestine, *6*:35–36, 38–41
    expulsion of Jews, *1*:28
    German attacks on, *3*:56
    reaction to Jewish refugees, *3*:23–24
    reaction to Nazi war crimes, *6*:26

Greek Jews
    persecution of, *5*:37, **38**, 39

Hermann Göring

videos about, *8*:58

Green, Gerald, *8*:41

Greenbaum, Clara, *6*:14

Greenfield, Howard, *8*:25

Grun, Max Von Der, *2*:13, 38; *3*:72

Gryn, Hugo, *6*:54

Grynszpan, Berta and Sendel, *2*:64

Grynszpan, Herschel, *2*:**64**; *3*:13

Gurdus, Luba, *8*:33

Gurock, Jeffrey S., *8*:13

Gurs concentration camp, *7*:37, 39–42

Gutman, Yisrael, *8*:7, 9, 19, 21–22

Gypsies. *See* Romani

H

Haakon VII, King of Norway, *3*:52

Haas, Gerta, *2*:53

Hacha, Emil, *3*:19–21

Hackett, David A., *8*:21

Haganah, *2*:53

Hallie, Phillip, *8*:25

Hamada, Carl, *3*:31

Hamerow, Theodore S., *8*:22

Harrison, Earl, *6*:21–23

Hasler, Alfred A., *8*:28

Hasselbach, Ingo, *6*:66

Hate groups, *6*:**60**, **65**–67

Heck, Alfons, *6*:61; *8*:36

Heine, Heinrich, *2*:13

Heller, Celia S., *8*:9

Himmler visits a POW camp in Minsk, USSR, 1941.

Heller, Clara, *2*:49; *3*:61

Heller, Elie, Emil, Frieda, Heshie, and Sholom, *2*:49

Hellman, Peter, *8*:25

Helmreich, William, *8*:36

Heretics, *1*:31

Hersh, Gizelle, *8*:33

Herzl, Theodor, *1*:44–45; *6*:35–36

Hess, Rudolf, *1*:56; *6*:**24**, 27

Heydrich, Reinhard, *4*:**11**
  death of, *4*:33, 60
  Nuremberg Trial investigation of, *3*:66
  plan for genocide, *3*:39, 42; *7*:31–32, 45
  role of *Einsatzgruppen*, *4*:16
  at Wannsee Conference, *4*:18–19
  See also SS (*Schutzstaffel*)

Hidden Child Foundation, *5*:70; *6*:58

Hilberg, Raoul, *3*:37; *7*:33; *8*:11, 19, 28

Hillsum, Etty, *8*:33
Himmler, Heinrich, *3*:**66**; *4*:**20**;
  5:**16**
  arrests of Jews, *2*:65
  ban on education, *3*:34–35
  creation of Bergen-Belsen
    concentration camp, *4*:45
  destruction of Warsaw ghetto,
    7:58
  liquidation of Jews in Eastern
    Europe, *4*:47–48, 51
  Lodz ghetto liquidation, *5*:49
  order to cease gassings, *5*:58
  organization of
    Einsatzgruppen, *4*:16
  reorganization of Reich
    Security Main Office,
    3:39
  role in deportation process,
    5:28
  role in planning genocide,
    3:67; *5*:10; *7*:51
  Sobibór revolt, *5*:22, 26
  Warsaw ghetto liquidation,
    4:68
  See also Gestapo; SS
    (*Schutzstaffel*)
Hindenburg, Paul von, *1*:**60**–61,
  63; *3*:11; *8*:48
Hirschmann, Chaim, *4*:28
History, Jewish
  beginning of Judaism,
    1:15–16
  chronology of, *1*:70–71
  early Roman Empire (27
    B.C.E. to circa 480 C.E.),
    1:17–19, 21

Middle Ages (500–1500 C.E.),
  1:22–31
modern era, early
  (1500s–1600s), *1*:35–37
1700s–1800s, *1*:37–45
World War I, *1*:50
Hitler, Adolf
  addressing German crowds,
    2:**8**; *7*:**7**
  addressing Reichstag, *1*:**68**
  annexation of Sudetenland,
    2:49; *3*:18, **59**, 60–61
  assassination plots against,
    5:48
  Beer Hall Rebellion, *1*:55
  at Berlin Olympics, *2*:**34**–38
  boycott of Jewish shops, *1*:63,
    64, 65; *7*:9–10, 17, 19
  childhood, *1*:53–54
  control over Europe, *5*:9
  declaring war on Poland,
    7:**30**
  decline of power, *5*:63
  development of antisemitism,
    1:54
  as hero of Skinheads, *6*:67
  inspecting damage from allied
    bombing, *5*:**56**
  invasion of Hungary, *5*:36
  Martin Luther's influence on,
    1:33
  master plan, *2*:27; *3*:15
  Mein Kampf, *1*:54, 56–**57**;
    2:66; *7*:8
  overview of role, *1*:9–10
  in prison, *1*:**52**
  at putsch trial, *1*:**55**

Adolf Hitler in prison, 1924.

reference books about, 8:15–18

reviewing Nazi troops, 2:**32**; 3:**13**; 8:**7**

rise to power, 1:59–63, **60**; 2:10–13; 3:10–11; 30

saluting Nazi youths, 3:**8**

suicide of, 5:72; 6:11

Third Reich, 1:51; 3:14 (map); 5:9

videos about, 8:46–49

view of Jewish "race," 1:11–13, 56–57; 2:20; 3:11; 4:18, 55; 5:43; 7:8–9

war on United States, 3:72

Zweites Buch, 7:9

See also Nazi Party; Nazis

Hitler Youth groups, 2:**15**, 24, 30, 37, 65; 6:9; 8:36

Hizme, Irene, 5:18

Holland, 1:36; 2:49; 3:53, 55, 57; 8:15, 50

Holocaust
  Association of Organizations, 6:72
  children of, 5:70; 6:57–58
  chronology of, 1:72
  definition of, 5:10–11
  denial of, 8:39
  general overview of, 8:6–7, 10–12, 45, 66, 69
  Martyrs' and Heroes' Remembrance Authority, 6:70
  proof of, 6:68–69
  specialized studies of, 8:38–39
  United States Memorial Museum, 1:43; 4:13; 5:35, 61; 6:33–34, 53, 71
  women of, 8:17, 22, 39

Homosexuals, persecution of, 2:48; 4:59, 63; 7:19; 8:30–31, 60

Hooray for Yiddish (Rosten), 1:39

Horowitz, Gordon, 8:29

Höss, Rudolf, 3:67

"Host desecration," 1:28

Hull, Cordell, 7:25

Hungary
  deportation of Jews in, 5:36–37; 7:61–64
  German invasion of, 5:36
  increasing violence against, 2:32–33; 5:36–37, 59

reference books about, *8*:10, 13

videos about, *8*:44

Hyman, Paula, *8*:9

I

I Am a Star (Auerbacher), *3*:24–26, 68

Illustrated books about the Holocaust, *8*:40–42

I Never Saw Another Butterfly (Fischl), *5*:40–41

Innocenti, Roberto, *8*:41

Irgun Brit Zion (ABZ), *5*:**29**; *6*:40

Isaac ben Daniel, *1*:24–25

Isabella, Queen of Spain, *1*:31

Israel, birth of, *6*:39–43; *7*:74

Italy, *2*:41–44; *5*:26–28; *8*:14, 34, 56, 58

J

Jackson, Robert, *6*:28, 30; *7*:73

Jan, Julius von, *2*:70

Jasphy, Pola, *5*:70–71

Jay, Martin, *8*:17

Jehovah's Witnesses, persecution of, *2*:46–48; *3*:33; *4*:59, 63–64; *7*:11–12; *8*:30–31, 59

Jerusalem
after World War II, *6*:39
destruction of, *1*:18; *6*:34
during religious Crusades, *1*:24

Jesus as viewed by Jews, *1*:12

Jewish Affairs, Department of, *4*:10, 46

Jewish Fighters Organization (ZOB), *4*:40–41, 67–72
See also resistance groups

Jewish Question—Material and its Treatment in Schools, The, *1*:67

Jews
after fall of Roman Empire, *1*:21
antisemitism during Middle Ages, *1*:26–28, 30–33
Ashkenazi, *1*:23, 39
birth of Israel, *6*:39–43; *7*:74
blaming of for "Black Death," *1*:30–31
centers of population 1500–1780, *1*:38 (map)
centers of population in Europe 1000s–1400s C.E., *1*:29 (map)
conspiracy theories about, *1*:36, 48
cremation of, *4*:16, 18, 27; *5*:55, 61; *7*:48–49
cultural traditions, *1*:19, 21, 41–43
death counts, *5*:69 (chart); *7*:59, 75 (chart)
deportations, *4*:**12**; *5*:**12**; *7*:**34**
after allied invasion of Europe, *5*:46–47, 49, 51 (map)
of children, *7*:51
description of, *4*:17–18; *7*:38–43, 46–50, 52–54

Yitzak Zuckerman and his wife Zivia Lubetkin, leaders of the ZOB.

from ghettos, *4*:38–39;
  5:16–17; *7*:52
goals of Wannsee
  Conference, *4*:18–19;
  7:45
of Hungarian Jews,
  5:36–37; *7*:61–64
increase of, *4*:19, 21, 25,
  27; *5*:**12**, 16–17 (map);
  7:34
"Operation Reinhard,"
  4:33
of Polish Jews, *3*:34;
  7:22–23, 48–49, 51
role of Gestapo, *2*:25;
  4:10

transit camps, *4*:**31**
  from Warsaw ghetto,
  4:38–39; *7*:52
in early modern era
  (1500s–1600s), *1*:35
emigration from Austria,
  2:58–59
emigration from Germany,
  1:65; *2*:27, 49, 71–72
  (graph); *3*:17–18; *7*:45,
  72
emigration to Palestine,
  6:35–39
expulsion from Germany
  during Middle Ages, *1*:28,
  31

extermination of
  Crimean Jews, *4*:19
  Finnish Jews, *4*:19
  French Jews, *5*:45
  Greek Jews, *5*:37, 39
  Hungarian Jews, *5*:36–37,
    59
  Italian Jews, *2*:42
  Polish Jews, *4*:60–61
gassing of, *4*:**20**
at Auschwitz–Birkenau con-
    centration camp, *4*:30, 51;
    5:49, 54–55, 58
at Belzec death camp, *4*:27
at Chelmno death camp,
4:16; *5*:19
in death camp showers,
    3:43; *5*:22
in gassing vans, *3*:64–65;
    4:**20**, 46–47; *5*:19
testing of Zyklon B gas,
    3:67–68
at Treblinka death camp,
    4:40
increasing violence against
  in Austria, *2*:32, 52–54;
    7:19–21
  in Czechoslovakia, *3*:21
  description of, *4*:18–19;
    7:12–13, 22–23

Young German Jews enjoy a trip to the beach, 1935.

in Greece, *5*:37–39

in Hungary, *2*:32–33

in Italy, *2*:41–44

Kristallnacht pogrom,
   2:65–70, **67**; *3*:9–10,
   13–14; *7*:23–25, 27–28

in Poland, *2*:32–33;
   3:35–36; *4*:60–61;
   7:18–19, 22–23, 30–31,
   51

during religious Crusades,
   1:24–26, **25**

in Romania, *2*:32–33

in 1700s–1800s, *1*:**34**;
   37–**40**

through propaganda, *2*:14,
   16–17

initial reaction to Hitler, *2*:12

intellectual contributions
   during Middle Ages, *1*:35

mass murders of
   due to "Black Death,"
      1:31
   due to Spanish
      Inquisition, *1*:37
   Nazi cover-ups, *7*:61
   Nazi plan for, *7*:51
   role of bystanders, 1:10
   through killing squads,
      1:43
   through pogroms, *7*:48
   United States' reaction to,
      7:57

medical experiments on,
   3:48; *5*:18

in Medieval Europe
   (500–1500 C.E.), *1*:22–31

A Jewish family from the Ukraine, 1935.

persecution of during
   religious Crusades, *1*:24–26

persecution of in Italy,
   2:41–44

population growth, *1*:16

pre-Holocaust, *8*:8–10, 43–44

reaction to Nuremberg Laws,
   2:21–22

resistance groups
   in Auschwitz–Birkenau
      concentration camp,
      5:55–58
   Bielski partisans, *4*:21–**22**;
      5:47–48; *8*:24
   description of partisan
      groups, *5*:28–30
   female, *8*:17

in ghettos, *4*:67–72; *8*:18, 54–55

Irgun Brit Zion (ABZ), *5*:**29**; *6*:40

Jewish Fighters Organization (ZOB), *4*:40–41, 67–72

location of uprisings, *5*:51 (map)

Raoul Wallenberg, *5*:**59**; *8*:25, 57–58

reference books about, *8*:17–18, 22–25

struggles of, *4*:28–29

underground, *2*:53; *4*:56; *5*:49–50; *8*:36, 53–54, 57

videos about, *8*:53–55, 57–58

in Warsaw ghetto, *4*:67–72

Roman domination of, *1*:18, 19 (map)

Russian persecution of in 1700s–1800s, *1*:**34**, 37–**40**

Sephardic, *1*:23

view of Jesus, *1*:12

Jews in Italy, The (Orano), *2*:42

Johnson, Cornelius, *2*:38

Judaism

development of, *1*:15–16

during early modern era (1500s–1600s), *1*:35

during Middle Ages (500–1500 C.E.), *1*:22–31

misclassification as a "race," *1*:11–13, 41, 56–57; *7*:15–18

split with Christianity, *1*:12

Judenrate

in Hungary, *5*:36–37

Members of the *Judenrat,* Cracow ghetto 1940.

reference books about, *8*:13,
19
role of, *3*:21; *7*:**32**–33
videos about, *8*:50
in Warsaw ghetto, *3*:45; *4*:36,
38–39; *7*:52

K

Kaes, Anton, *8*:17
Kahane, David, *4*:48–49
Kaltenbrunner, Ernst, *6*:28
Kalter, Joachim, *7*:**22**–24,
48–49, 65–66
Kantor, Alfred, *8*:42
Kaplan, Chaim, *3*:49, 51
Karski, Jan, *3*:34
Karthaus, Wolfgang, *2*:53
Kater, Michael H., *8*:17, 29
Katz, Jacob, *8*:37
Kaufering concentration camp,
7:66
Keibel, Jane, *7*:**28**–29
Keitel, Wilhelm, *6*:**25**
Keller, Ulrich, *4*:72
Keneally, Thomas, *5*:31
Kennedy, John F., *7*:25
Kennedy, Joseph, *7*:25
Keren, Nili, *8*:10
Khmer Rouge, *6*:63–64
Kieler, Jorgen, *5*:23
Killing centers. *See* death
camps
Killing squads. *See*
Einsatzgruppen
Kindertransport, *7*:27–28
Kirschenblatt-Gimblett,

Barbara, *8*:8
KKK (Ku Klux Klan), *6*:**65**
Klanwatch, *6*:65–66
Klarsfeld, Beate and Serge,
6:48–51
Klee, Ernst, *8*:29
Klein, Gerda Weissman, *8*:33
Klein-Pollack, Cecilie, *6*:58
Kluger, Ruth, *3*:54
Knochen, Helmuth, *3*:58
Kogen, Eugen, *8*:21
Koonz, Claudia, *8*:17
Korczak, Janusz, *4*:41; *7*:52;
8:49
Kotouc, Kurt Jiri, *8*:34
Krakowski, Shmuel, *8*:22, 28
Kratzau Women's Labor Camp,
6:17
Kristallnacht, *2*:65–70, **67**;
3:9–10, 13–14; *7*:23–25,
27–28
Krizkova, Maria Rut, *8*:34
Krzepicki, Abraham Jacob,
4:48–49
Kuglemass, Jack, *8*:9

L

Labor camps. *See* concentra-
tion camps
Langer, Lawrence L., *8*:39
Laredo Bru, Federico, *3*:24
Laska, Vera, *8*:22
Latour, Anny, *8*:22
Latvia, *8*:13–14
Laws, anti-Jewish. *See*
Nuremberg Laws

Shattered shopwindows in Berlin after *Kristallnacht*, 1938.

Lazare, Bernard, *1*:11, 16
Lazare, Lucien, *8*:25
Le Chambon (France), *7*:41–43;
    8:25, 59
LeChen, Evelyn, *6*:15
Lee, Kathleen, *8*:26
Leiber, Frajdla, *4*:51
Leitner, Isabella, *8*:34, 36
Lessner, Baron von, *2*:46
Lester, Eleanor, *8*:25
Levi, Primo, *5*:27; *8*:21, 34, 67
Levin, Avraham, *7*:52
Levin, Dov, *8*:23
Levin, Nora, *8*:11
Liberation, *5*:65 (map), **68**; *6*:13
    of Auschwitz–Birkenau,

5:60–61; *6*:11
    of Bergen-Belsen, *5*:69–70;
      6:14
    of Buchenwald, *5*:64–66;
      6:11, 15; *7*:69
    of Dachau, *5*:**68**, 70–71; *6*:11,
      16; *7*:69–71; *8*:60
    description of survivors,
      6:**12**–14, **15**, **18**; *7*:69,
      71–72
    of Kratzau, *6*:17
    of Mauthausen, *6*:14–15
    of Ohrdruf, *5*:63; *6*:15–16
    problems of survivors, *6*:17,
      19–23
    of Ravensbrück, *5*:71–72

reference books about, *8*:7,
31–32, 37
by Soviet Army, *6*:9–11
of Theresienstadt, *6*:16
videos about, *8*:45, 60–61,
63–64
web sites about, *8*:69
Lichtenberg, Bernhard, *2*:70
Lidice, Czechoslovakia, *4*:33
Liebmann, Hanne Hirsch, *7*:10,
38–43
Liebschutz Rosza, Lisa, *3*:20, 26
"Lightning War" with Poland,
3:27, 29–32; *4*:60; *7*:30–31

Lipson, Alfred, *7*:**18**–19
Lipson, Carol Frenkel, *4*:43
Lipstadt, Deborah, *8*:39
Lithuania, *1*:42–43; *8*:23
Livingston, Ellen, *1*:42
Lochner, Irmgard, *2*:24–25
Lodz ghetto, *3*:43–**46**, **63**; *4*:**36**,
46; *7*:**36**; *8*:**68**
children of, *7*:58
liquidation of, *5*:49
reference books about,
8:18–19, 35, 38
videos about, *8*:49–50
See also ghettos

Liberation at Allach, a sub-camp of Dachau, 1945.

Lubetkin, Zivia, *4*:**41**, 69–70
Lukas, Richard, *4*:60
Luther, Martin, *1*:32–**33**
Lux, Stefan, *2*:33
Luxembourg, German invasion
    of, *3*:53

M

Majdanek death camp, *5*:19,
    32; *8*:32
Manhattan Project, *2*:44; *3*:27
Mann, Peggy, *8*:33
Mann, Thomas, *2*:13
Mansbacher, Herta, *2*:67
Margulies, Fred, *7*:12–13
Marr, Wilhelm, *1*:11
Marriage bans, *2*:20–21;
    7:15–17
Marrin, Albert, *8*:17
Marrus, Michael R., *8*:7, 14, 29
Martarda (ship), *7*:72
"Master Race," *1*:41; *3*:42
Mauthausen labor camp, *4*:**50**,
    54; *6*:14–15; *8*:53
Mayer, Helene, *2*:37
Medical examinations, *2*:22
Medical experiments per-
    formed on Jews, *3*:48; *5*:18
Medieval Europe. *See* Middle
    Ages
Meed, Vladka, *8*:23, 34
Mein Kampf (Hitler), *1*:54,
    56–**57**; *2*:66; *7*:8
Meir, Golda, *2*:57
Melson, Robert, *6*:62
Meltzer, Milton, *8*:26

Memoirs, *8*:9, 21, 32–35,
    61–64, 67
Mendelsohn, Ezra, *8*:9
Mengele, Josef, *5*:18, 54; *6*:**44**,
    48; *7*:55
Mentally disabled people, per-
    secution of, *3*:42–43; *4*:59,
    63; *7*:10, 33–34; *8*:30–31
Metcalfe, Ralph, *2*:38
Metzen, Frieda, *3*:33
Meyers, Sondra, *8*:26
Michaelis, Meir, *8*:14
Middle Ages (500–1500 C.E.)
    antisemitism during,
        1:26–28, 30–33
    "Black Death," *1*:30–31
    Judaism during, *1*:22–31
    religious Crusades, *1*:24–26
Military buildup in Germany,
    2:12, 27, 45
Miller, Richard L., *8*:29
Mills, Eric, *2*:23
Milton, Sybil, *8*:40, 42
Moise, Maria Sava, *4*:62
Molotov, Vyacheslav, *3*:**16**
Mommsen, Hans, *8*:17
Money lenders, Jewish,
    1:23–24
Morely, John F., *8*:30
Morgenthau, Henry, *4*:53
Mosse, George, *8*:18
Müller, Filip, *4*:30; *5*:55
Müller, Heinrich, *6*:46
Munich
    Hitler's march on, *1*:55
    Pact, *2*:60
Murders, mass Jewish

Benito Mussolini shakes Neville Chamberlain's hand at the Munich Conference, 1938.

due to "Black Death," *1*:31
due to Spanish Inquisition,
  1:37
Nazi cover-ups, *7*:61
Nazi plan for, *7*:51
role of bystanders, *1*:10
through killing squads, *1*:43;
  3:64–67; *4*:9
through pogroms, *7*:48
United States' reaction to,
  7:57
Murders, ritual, *1*:26–28
Murrow, Edward, *5*:64
Museums, *8*:71–77
Mussolini, Benito, *2*:41–43, **61**;
  3:17, 30, 59; *5*:26; *8*:14

N
National Socialist German
  Workers' Party. *See* Nazi
  Party
Naumann, Abraham, *4*:47
Nazi hunters, *6*:46–51
Nazi Party, *1*:**54**, **62**; *8*:17,
  46–47
  boycott of Jewish shops,
    1:63, **64**, 65; *7*:9–10, 17,
    19
  collaborators, *5*:**57**; *8*:27–30
  criminal hunters, *6*:46–51
  decline of power, *5*:63, 72
  escape of members after

World War II, *6*:45, 50
founding of, *1*:54; *3*:11
goals of, *3*:39, 42, 67;
    4:10–11; *5*:10; *7*:8, 31–32,
    45, 51
growth of power, *1*:62, 65;
    2:10–17, 24, 27; *5*:10
influence on German
    Parliament, *1*:59
influence on schools, *2*:15,
    23–24, 30–32, 43; *7*:12
march on Munich, *1*:55
surrender of, *6*:16
use of propaganda, *5*:40; *7*:35
war crimes, *6*:25–31; *7*:73
See also Hitler, Adolf
Nazis
    attack on Warsaw ghetto,

4:38–39, 67–72; *7*:58–59
attempts to erase evidence,
    6:10; *7*:61
deportation of Jews
    after allied invasion of
        Europe, *5*:46–47, 49, 51
        (map)
    to Belzec death camp, *4*:27
    in Czechoslovakia, *3*:26
    definition of, *4*:10
    description of, *7*:46–47,
        49–50, 53–54
    by *Einsatzgruppen*,
        4:16–18
    to France, *7*:38–43
    goals of Wannsee
        Conference, *4*:18–19;
        7:45

An early photo of the Nazi Party in Germany, 1922.

in Hungary, *5*:36–37;
  7:61–64
increase of, *4*:19–21, 25;
  5:**12**, 16–17 (map); *7*:**34**
"Operation Reinhard,"
  4:33
in Poland, *2*:63–64; *3*:34;
  4:60; *7*:22–23, 48–49,
  51–52
to Sobibór, *4*:30–31
via trains, *5*:27–28;
  7:38–39, 63–64
from Warsaw ghetto,
  4:38–39; *7*:52
destruction of synagogues,
  2:**40**, 68 (map)
in Berlin, *2*:**62**, 67
in Italy, *2*:**40**
during *Kristallnacht*, *2*:67;
  7:**24**
in Munich, *2*:58
in Nuremberg, *2*:58
in Poland, *4*:**58**; *7*:30–31
gassing of Jews
  at Auschwitz–Birkenau
  concentration camp, *4*:30,
  51; *5*:49, 54–55, 58
  at Belzec death camp,
  4:27
  at Chelmno death camp,
  4:16
  children, *5*:49, 54–55
  in death camp showers,
  3:43; *5*:22
  description of, *3*:43
  testing of Zyklon B gas,
  3:43, 67–68

at Treblinka death camp,
  4:40
in vans, *3*:64–65; *4*:**20**,
  46–47; *5*:19
German public reaction to,
  2:25–26; *4*:10; *5*:13, 67
invasion of
  Austria, *2*:51–52, 54; *3*:13;
  4:55; *7*:19–**21**
  Belgium, *2*:49; *3*:53
  Czechoslovakia, *2*:49,
  60–61; *3*:15, 18–21, 26
  European countries,
  2:41–42; *4*:9, 14 (map);
  5:9
  France, *3*:56–57
  Great Britain, *3*:56
  Hungary, *5*:36
  Norway, *3*:52–53
  Poland, *3*:27, 29–32; *4*:60;
  7:30–31
  Rhineland, *2*:30–31
  Soviet Union, *3*:59, 64; *4*:19
killing of French Jews, *5*:45
murder of non-Jews, *1*:10;
  4:32, 48; *5*:19
organized attacks on Jews,
  2:65–68; *3*:13
persecution of Polish Jews,
  4:60–61; *7*:22–23, 30–31,
  51
resistance groups against,
  5:**29**, **48**
  armed, *8*:22–24
  in Auschwitz–Birkenau
  concentration camp,
  5:55–58

Hitler addresses the Reichstag, 1939.

Bielski partisans, *4*:21–**22**; *5*:47–48; *8*:24

female, *8*:17

in ghettos, *8*:18, 54–55

Jewish Fighters Organization (ZOB), *4*:40–41, 67–72

location of uprisings, *5*:51 (map)

non-Jews, *8*:53

Raoul Wallenberg, *5*:**59**; *8*:25, 57–58

reference books about, *8*:17–18, 22–25

in Sobibór death camp, *5*:22–23, 25–26

struggles of, *4*:28–29

underground, *2*:53; *4*:56; *5*:49–50; *8*:36; 53–54; 57

videos about, *8*:53–55; 57–58

in Warsaw ghetto, *4*:67–72

"White Rose," *4*:63–**65**; *8*:23

treatment of elderly Jews, *4*:25–26

See also Hitler, Adolf

Nazism

reference books about, *8*:8, 10–18, 27–30, 39

videos about, *8*:45, 47–48, 59

Neave, Airy, *6*:27–28

Neo-Nazi Party, *6*:**60**, 66–67

Netherlands, Jewish influence on, *1*:36

Nicholas II, Czar of Russia, *1*:40

Niemöller, Martin, *1*:10; *2*:48

"Night of Broken Glass." *See Kristallnacht*

"Night of the Long Knives," *2*:42

Night (Wiesel), *6*:56; *7*:64–65

Non-Jews

deaths of, *1*:10; *4*:32, 48; *5*:19

persecution of

homosexuals, *2*:48; *4*:59, 63; *7*:19; *8*:30–31, 60

Jehovah's Witnesses, *2*:46–48; *3*:33; *4*:59, 63–64; *7*:11–12; *8*:30–31, 59

mentally and physically handicapped, *3*:42–43; *4*:59, 63; *7*:10, 33–34; *8*:30–31

in Poland, *4*:48, 59

reference books about, *8*:7, 26, 30–31

Romani, *2*:**47**–48; *3*:**48**; *4*:59, 61–63; *7*:**11**–12; *8*:30, 59

Soviet prisoners of war, *4*:59, 63

students, *4*:32

videos about, *8*:59–60

reluctance to help Jews, *3*:37; *5*:43–44

rescue attempts, *5*:23; *8*:24–27, 55–56

resistance fighters, *4*:32, 63–65; *7*:21, 41–43; *8*:23; 53

A group of Romani awaits instructions at Belzec concentration camp, 1942.

Noren, Catherine, 8:10

Normandy invasion, 5:44–46; 6:10

See also allied forces

Norway, 3:52–53; 8:12, 58

Novak, Zdenka, 5:28–30

November Pogroms (*Kristallnacht*), 2:65–70; 3:9–10, 13–14; 7:23–25, 27–28

Novitsch, Miriam, 8:42

Nuremberg Laws, 1:69; 2:19–23; 3:12–13, 36, 48; 7:15–18

Nuremberg Trials, 3:66; 6:**24**–31; 7:**73**; 8:**31**–32

O

ODESSA, 6:45

Ofer, Dalia, 8:26

Ogilvie-Forbes, Sir George, 2:70

Ohrdruf concentration camp, 5:63–64; 6:11, 15–16

Oliner, Samuel, 8:26

Olympic Games of 1936, 2:35–39; 8:48

One By One, 6:58

Operation Barbarossa, 5:43

"Operation Reinhard," 4:33

Orano, Paolo, 2:42

Ornest, Zdenek, *8*:34
Orphans, Jewish, *6*:19
Ottoman Empire, *1*:31, 45
Ovazza, Ettore, *2*:42–43
Ovazza, Franca, *2*:43–44
Owens, Jesse, *2*:38, **39**

P

"Pale of Settlement," Russian,
   1:37–40, 41 (map)
Palestine
   birth of Jewish state of
      Israel, *6*:39–43; *7*:74
   emigration of Jews, *3*:23,
      54; *4*:23; *6*:23, 35–39, 42;
      7:72
   history of, *1*:16–17; *8*:26
   as Jewish homeland,
      1:44–45
Paris, Matthew, *1*:28
Parker, Leonard, *6*:16
Partisan groups. *See* resistance
   groups

Nuremberg trial, 1945

Passover, *1*:26, **45**
Patterson, Charles, *8*:37
Patton, George, *5*:64, 66–67;
   6:11
Paxton, Robert O., *8*:14, 29
Pearl Harbor, *3*:71
Pelt, Robert Jan van, *8*:20
Perpetrators, *8*:21, 27–32
Persian Empire, *1*:17, 19 (map)
Petain, Marshal, *3*:57
Peter the Hermit, *1*:24
Plague, bubonic, *1*:29–31
Plant, Richard, *8*:31
Pobedonostsev, Konstantin,
   1:39
Pogroms
   definition of, *2*:14
   increase of, *7*:48–49
   Kristallnacht, *2*:65–70, **67**;
      3:9–10, 13–14; *7*:23–25,
      27–28
   against Polish Jews, *4*:60
   after World War II, *6*:22–23;
      7:72
Pohl, Willi, *7*:**12**
Poland
   citizenship laws, *2*:63–64;
      7:22
   deportation of Jews,
      2:63–64; *3*:34; *4*:60;
      7:22–23, 48–49, 51–52
   destruction of synagogues,
      4:**58**; *7*:30–31
   German invasion of, *3*:27,
      29–32; *4*:60; *7*:30–31
   growth of antisemitism, *2*:33;
      4:60–61; *7*:18–19

increasing violence in,
2:32–33; 3:35–36; 7:18–19,
22–23
Jewish culture, 3:31
Jewish death counts, 4:47
Nazification of, 3:34–37
persecution of non-Jews in,
4:48, 59
pogroms after World War II,
6:22–23; 7:72
reference books about,
8:8–9, 22, 35
videos about, 8:44, 55
Poliakov, Leon, 1:11; 8:38
Pol Pot, 6:64
Porat, Dina, 8:14
Potasinski, Lee, 7:**30**–31, 46–47,
53–57, 66–67, **69**–71
Poverty, Jewish, 2:29–30, 45
Probst, Christopher, 4:63–65
Propaganda against Jews,
2:13–14, 20; 5:40; 7:35
Protestant Reformation, 1:32
*Protocols of the Elders of Zion,
The*, 1:36, 48–50, **49**

R

Rabinowitz, Dorothy, 8:37
Racial discrimination, 2:12, 20,
22, 36, 38, 43
See also antisemitism; Hitler,
Adolf; homosexuals;
Jehovah's Witnesses;
mentally disabled; Nazi
Party; Nazis; Romani
Radom ghetto, 8:**39**

Ramati, Alexander, 8:26
Rautkallio, Hannu, 8:14
Ravensbrück women's camp,
5:71–72
Reck-Malleczewen, Friedrich
Percyval, 2:39
Red Cross, 5:40; 7:41–42
Red Friday, 3:65
Reference books about
antisemitism, 8:37–38
concentration and extermination camps, 8:20–21
country/cultural studies,
8:12–15
European Jewry before the
Holocaust, 8:8–10
Germany, Hitler and the Rise
of Nazism, 8:15–18
ghettos, 8:18–19
liberation and judgment,
8:31–32
memoirs and diaries, 8:9, 21,
32–35
non-Jewish victims, 8:30–31
overview of Holocaust, 8:6–8,
10–12
perpetrators, bystanders and
collaborators, 8:27–30
rescues, 8:24–27
resistance, 8:22–24
specialized studies, 8:38–39
survivors, 8:6, 9, 15, 19–20,
25–26, 32–34, 36–37
Reformation, Protestant, 1:32
Refugees, Jewish
after World War II, 6:23

Matzah is baked in the Lodz ghetto, 1940.

assistance by the Haganah,
2:53

in Czechoslovakia, 3:26

emigration numbers by
countries, 2:58, 72 (chart);
3:22

Evian Conference, 2:**56**, **57**;
3:22; 4:53; 7:22

foreign countries refusals to
admit, 2:59; 3:18, 22; 4:23;
6:23; 7:25, 28–29

in France, 7:37

in Palestine, 3:54; 4:23

reaction by America to,
2:56–59; 3:23, 25; 4:23,
53

reaction by Great Britain to,
3:23–24

Salvador (ship), sinking of,
3:62

on *St. Louis* (ship), 3:24–**25**;
7:28–29

Reich Citizenship Laws,
2:19–23

Reichstag building, burning of,
1:60–**61**

Reinharz, Jehuda, 8:9

Reiss, Johanna, 8:34

Religion
development of Judaism,
1:15–16

Jewish-Christian split, 1:12, 22

Jewishness, misclassification
as a "race," *1*:11–13, 41,
56–57
Nazi opposition to, *3*:33
rituals, *1*:26–28
Rescues, *5*:**22**, 23; *8*:12, 24–27,
55–56, 58, 68
See also Le Chambon; Righteous
Gentiles; Schindler, Oskar;
Wallenberg, Raoul
Resettlement of Jews. *See*
deportations
Resistance groups, *5*:**29**, **48**
armed, *8*:22–24
in Auschwitz–Birkenau concentration camp, *5*:55–58
Bielski partisans, *4*:21–**22**;
5:47–48; *8*:24
female, *8*:17
in ghettos, *8*:18, 54–55
Jewish Fighters Organization
(ZOB), *4*:40–41, 67–72
location of uprisings, *5*:51 (map)
non-Jews, *8*:53
Raoul Wallenberg, *5*:**59**;
8:25, 57–58
reference books about, *8*:7,
17–18, 22–25
in Sobibór death camp,
5:22–23, 25–26
struggles of, *4*:28–29
underground, *5*:49–50;
8:53–54
videos about, *8*:53–55;
57–58
"White Rose," *4*:63–**65**; *8*:23
Resource centers, *8*:71–77

Danish fishermen rescue Jews, circa 1943.

Revolts, Jewish. *See* resistance
groups
Rhineland
attack by Peter the Hermit,
1:24–25
German invasion of, *2*:30–31
videos on, *8*:47
Ribbentrop, Joachim von, *2*:71;
3:**16**; *6*:24; 27–28
Riegner, Gerhart, *7*:57
Riga ghetto, *8*:19
Righteous Gentiles, *6*:70; *7*:21;
8:34–35, 62
See also Le Chambon; rescues; resistance groups;

Schindler, Oskar;
Wallenberg, Raoul; "White
Rose"
Ringelblum, Emanuel,
4:36–37, 39, 61, 68; *7*:**36**;
8:19
Ripka, Hubert, *3*:68
Rittner, Carol, *8*:26, 39
Ritual murders, *1*:26–28
Roehm, Ernst, *1*:55; *4*:63
Roman domination over
Hebrews, *1*:18, 19 (map)
Romani, persecution of,
2:**47**–48; *3*:**48**; *4*:59, 61–63;
7:**11**–12; *8*:30, 59
Romania, *2*:32–33; *8*:44
Rome-Berlin Axis, *2*:41
Roosevelt, Eleanor, *6*:22
Roosevelt, Franklin D.
authorization for building
atomic bomb, *3*:27
debate over Jewish refugees,
3:23, 25
establishment of War
Refugee Board, *4*:53
initiation of Evian
Conference, *2*:56; *3*:22
lack of opposition to Hitler,
5:13
reaction to *Kristallnacht*,
2:70
reaction to Pearl Harbor
invasion, *3*:71
request for Nazi war crime
trials, *6*:26
Rose, Leesha, *3*:53, 62
Rosenbaum, Alan S., *8*:31

Rosenberg, Alfred, *6*:27
Rosenberg, Maxine B., *8*:26
Rosenthal, Avram and
Emmanuel, *5*:**24**
Rossell, Seymour, *8*:12
Rosten, Leo, *1*:39
Roth, John K., *8*:39
Roth-Hanno, Renee, *8*:34
Rothschild, Lionel de, *1*:36;
6:36
Routes to Roots, *6*:58
Rowecki, Stefan, *4*:60
Rubenstein, Richard, *8*:39
Russia
Czar Alexander II, *1*:39
Czarina Catherine, *1*:37
Czar Nicholas II, *1*:40

Emanuel Ringelblum

"Pale of Settlement," *1*:37–40, 41 (map)

persecution of Jews in 1700s–1800s, *1*:**34**, 37–**40**

See also Soviet Union

S

Sachar, Abram, *6*:40

Sachs, Alexander, *3*:27

Sachsenhausen concentration camp, *2*:68–69

Salvador (ship), sinking of, *3*:62

SA (*Sturmabteilungen*), *2*:16, 65; *3*:11; *7*:10

Sauvage, Pierre, *5*:44

Scandinavian countries, German invasion of, *3*:52–53

Scaria (ship), *6*:37

Schindler, Oskar, *5*:**31**

Schindler's List (Keneally), *5*:31

Schmitz, Richard, *2*:46

Schneider, Gertrude, *8*:15, 19

Scholl, Hans and Sophie, *4*:63–**65**

Scholl, Inge, *8*:23

Schools
antisemitism in, *1*:38, 67

Holocaust teachings in, *6*:69

Nazi influence on, *2*:15, 23–24, 30–32; *7*:12

in Warsaw ghetto, *4*:37

Schuschnigg, Kurt von, *2*:51–52

Seder, Passover, *1*:**45**

Seltzer, Robert, *1*:16–17, 19

Sender, Ruth, *8*:35

Sened, Alexander, *8*:19

Sephardic Jews, *1*:23

Seyss-Inquart, Arthur, *3*:57

Shanghai, Jewish asylum in, *3*:22

Sherrow, Victoria, *8*:15

Shirer, William, *2*:53; *3*:21

Shmeruk, Chone, *8*:9

Shneiderman, S. L., *8*:35

Short, Dewey, *5*:66

Shtetls, *1*:37, 42–**43**; *6*:33–34; *8*:44, 64

Shulman, William L., *6*:72

Silkes, G., *4*:37

Silver, Eric, *8*:27

Skinheads, *6*:66–67

Slotkin, Rene, *5*:18

Snyder, Louis L., *8*:18

Sobibór death camp, *4*:30–32; *5*:19, 22–23, 25–26

Son, Kitei, *2*:38

Oskar Schindler

Public humiliation of elderly Jews on a Warsaw street, circa 1940.

Sonderkommando revolt,
   5:55–58, 60
Sonenson, Yaffa, *6*:34
Sonnenmark, Thea, *2*:54;
   7:**20**–21, **24**–25
Sosnowski, Piotr, *3*:33
Soviet Army, *5*:58, 60–61;
   6:9–11; *7*:65
Soviet Union, *8*:13
   German invasion of, *3*:59
   non-aggression pact with
      Hitler, *3*:26–27, 31
   See also Russia
Spain, *8*:12
Spanish Inquisition, *1*:**20**, 31

"Special Detail" revolt,
   5:55–58, 60
"Special Duty" Squads,
   3:41–42, 64–67; *5*:55–58, 60
Spector, Shmuel, *8*:28
Speer, Albert, *6*:31
Spielberg, Steven, *6*:68–69
SS (*Schutzstaffel*), *1*:**58**
   attack on Warsaw ghetto,
      4:69–72; *7*:58–59
   control over Hungary, *5*:36
   death marches, *6*:15
   description of abuses by,
      2:54, 69
Einsatzgruppen, *4*:**8**, **17**

Jewish passengers in Havana harbor, on the S.S. *St. Louis* in 1939.

establishment of, *3*:41–42

mass murders by, *1*:43; *3*:64–67; *4*:9

orders from Reinhard Heydrich, *7*:31

overview of role, *4*:16–18

use of gassing vans, *3*:64–65; *4*:**20**, 46–47; *5*:19

evacuation of concentration camps, *6*:15

overthrowing of at Auschwitz–Birkenau, *5*:56

resistance against, *4*:28–29, 65

role of, *2*:25; *3*:41–42, 64–67; *4*:10, 16–18; *5*:10

sheltering of after World War II, *6*:45

union with Gestapo, *2*:51

at Wannsee Conference, *4*:19

war crimes, *6*:25–31; *7*:73

See also Gestapo

St. Louis (ship), *3*:24–25; *7*:28–29

Stadtler, Bea, *8*:23

Stalin, Josef, *3*:16; *6*:63

Stangl, Franz, *6*:47, 51

Star of David, *3*:21, 37, 68; *4*:**62**; *7*:35

Stauffenberg, Claus, *5*:48

Stein, Andre, *8*:27

Steinmuller, Johann, *4*:56

Sterilization, *2*:21; *3*:42; *7*:10–11

Stern Gang, *6*:40

Stobierski, Mieczyslaw, *5*:61

Stoller, Sam, *2*:38

Strasser, Anna, *4*:55

Strasshoff concentration camp, *7*:63

Streicher, Julius, *1*:**54**; *2*:58; *7*:13, 16–17

Stroop, Jürgen, *4*:69–70, 72; *7*:59
Struma (ship), sinking of,
  3:71; *4*:23; *6*:37
Sudetenland, Hitler's
  annexation of, *2*:49, **59**,
  60–61; *3*:18
Suhl, Yuri, *8*:23
Suicide of Jews, *2*:33, 39, 44,
  46, 55; *4*:39, 71
Survival in Auschwitz (Levi), *5*:27
Survivors
  children, *6*:57–58
  current needs of, *6*:53–55,
    58–59
  description of upon liberation, *6*:**12**–14, **15**, **18**;
  7:69, 71–72
illustrated books about, *8*:42
legacy of, *4*:11; *5*:70–71
problems of upon liberation,
  6:17, 19–23
reference books about, *8*:6,
  9, 15, 19–20, 25–26,
  32–34, 36–37
videos about, *8*:50–52,
  56–57, 60, 63–64
web sites about, *8*:66, 69
Survivors of the Shoah Visual
  History Foundation, *6*:68–69
Sutzkever, Abraham, *6*:28–29

Arrivals at Westerbork transit camp, circa 1942.

Swastikas, *1*:**68**; *2*:15, 67
Sweden, *8*:24, 58
Switzerland, *8*:28
Synagogues, destruction of,
    2:**40**, 68 (map)
    in Berlin, *2*:**62**, 67
    in Italy, *2*:**40**
    during *Kristallnacht*, *2*:67; *7*:24
    in Munich, *2*:58
    in Nuremberg, *2*:58
    in Poland, *4*:**58**; *7*:30–31
Syrkin, Marie, *8*:23

Szilard, Leo, *3*:27
Szner, Zvi, *8*:19

T

Tattoos, *4*:43–44; *6*:**57**
Taylor, Telford, *8*:32
Tec, Nechama, *8*:24, 27, 35
Tenenbaum, Joseph, *7*:72
Theresienstadt concentration
    camp, *5*:39
    description of, *5*:40; *7*:49–50

Boys from the Warsaw ghetto, 1939

general overview of, *5*:40
illustrated books about, *8*:41–42
liberation of, *6*:16
reference books about, *8*:32, 34
treatment of elderly, *4*:25–26
videos about, *8*:52
Third Reich, *2*:10, 51; *4*:9
beginning of, *1*:60
collapse of, *6*:9–11
definition of, *1*:51
Thompson, Vivian Alpert, *8*:42
Toll, Nelly S., *8*:35
Torahs, *1*:16
Torquemada, Tomas de, *1*:31
T-4 Program, *3*:42–43
Trains, deportation, *5*:27–28;
7:38–39, 63–64
Transit camps, *4*:**31**; *5*:27; *7*:70;
8:**34**, 50
Treaty of Versailles, *1*:50–51; *2*:10–11,
27, 31; *3*:10–11, 18; *6*:26
Treblinka death camp, *4*:40; *5*:22
Trocme, Andre, *5*:44
Trocme, Magda, *5*:44; *7*:43
Troper, Harold, *8*:27
Truman, Harry, *6*:21–23
Trunk, Isaiah, *8*:19
Turkish Empire, *1*:31, 45
Typhus epidemic, *3*:63–64;
5:68–70; *6*:16

u

Underground defense groups,
2:53; *4*:56; *5*:49–50; *8*:36,
53–54, 57
See also resistance groups

Unemployment of Jews,
2:29–30
Unger, Aviva, *5*:15–16
United Nations
creation of Israel,
6:39–40
stand on crimes against
humanity, *6*:31; *7*:74
United States
antisemitism in, *2*:32
Hitler's declaration of war
on, *3*:72
Holocaust Memorial
Museum, *1*:43; *4*:13;
5:35, 61; *6*:33–34, 53,
71

Hitler inspects bombing damage in Germany, 1944.

A father and son await deportation with others in Cracow, 1941.

reaction to
  crisis in Palestine, *6*:38–39
  Jewish deportations, *7*:34
  Jewish massacre, *7*:57
  Jewish refugees, *2*:56–59;
    3:23, 25; *4*:23, 53
  Nazi boycott of Jewish
    shops, *1*:63
  Nazi war crimes, *6*:11,
    21–22, 26, 45–46
reference books on, *8*:28,
  30, 39
role as bystander, *2*:23; *5*:13
threat to boycott Berlin
  Olympics, *2*:36–37

Untermenschen, *3*:41; *4*:14, 16;
  5:9–10
Uprisings, *5*:51 (map)
  in Auschwitz–Birkenau
    concentration camp, *5*:55–58
  in Bialystok ghetto, *5*:17
  reference books about, *8*:22,
    24
  in Sobibór death camp,
    5:22–23, 25–26
  videos about, *8*:55
  in Vilnius ghetto, *5*:16–17
  in Warsaw ghetto, *4*:68–**72**,
    71; *7*:58–59
Urban II, Pope, *1*:24–26

A member of the underground resistance sets a dynamite charge on a railway near Vilnius, 1943.

Gas van near Chelmno

V

Van der Lubbe, Marinus, *1*:60–61

Vans, gassing, *3*:64–65; *4*:**20**, 46–47; *5*:19

V-E Day (Victory in Europe Day), *6*:13

Versailles, Treaty of, *1*:50–51; *2*:10–11, 27, 31; *3*:10–11, 18; *6*:26

Videos about
    concentration and extermina-
        tion camps, *8*:50–53
European Jewry before the
    Holocaust, *8*:43–44
Germany, Hitler, and the rise
    of Nazism, *8*:46–49
liberation, *8*:60–61
memoirs, *8*:61–64
non-Jewish victims, *8*:59–60
overview of Holocaust, *8*:45
rescues, *8*:55–59
resistance, *8*:53–55
Vilnius ghetto, *5*:16; *7*:61; *8*:18, 54

Volavkova, Hana, *8*:42
Vom Rath, Ernst, *2*:64, 71

W

Wallenberg, Raoul, *5*:**59**; *8*:25,
57–58
Wannsee Conference, *4*:18–19,
46; *7*:45–46; *8*:68
Warsaw ghetto, *3*:**40**, **49**; *4*:**34**;
7:**37**, **52**; *8*:**41**
children of, *4*:**34**, 36–38, 41;
7:52
description of, *3*:44–47;

4:35–36; *7*:36
liquidation of, *4*:38–41, 48,
66, 67–72
reference books about, *8*:19,
22–24, 32, 34–35
schools in, *4*:37
smuggling in, *4*:**37**–38
uprising in, *4*:68–**72**, **71**;
7:58–59
videos about, *8*:49–50,
54–55, 64
See also ghettos
Waterford, Helen, *6*:54; *8*:36
Wdowinsky, David, *4*:37

A survivor from Buchenwald confronts a former prison guard after liberation, 1945.

60

Raoul Wallenberg

Web sites, 8:65–69
Weglun, Walter, 2:31
Weihs, Erika, 2:54
Weimar government, 1:50–51, 59; 7:11; 8:17
Weiner, Miriam, 6:58
Weiss, John, 8:18
Weissova-Hoskova, Helga, 4:25
Weizmann, Chaim, 6:36
Werfel, Franz, 3:58
Westerbork transit camp, 4:31; 8:34, 50
"White Paper," 3:23; 6:37

"White Rose," 4:63–**65**; 8:23
See also resistance groups
White supremacist groups, 6:**60**, **65**–67
Wiechert, Ernst, 2:25–26
Wiesel, Elie, 5:13, 64–65; 6:**56**; 7:64–65; 8:21, 35
Wiesenthal, Simon, 6:**47**
components of genocide, 6:62, 65
description of Dr. Josef Mengele, 5:18
Nazi hunter activities of, 6:46–48, 50–51, 59
report on Polish hatred of Jews, 4:60–61
report on survivors, 4:52
The Sunflower: On the Possibilities and Limits of Forgiveness, 8:32
Wigoder, Geoffrey, 8:7
Wilde, Georg, 2:69
Wilhelmina, Queen of Holland, 3:53
Williams, Lyle, 5:71
Wilner, Aryeh, 4:71
Wise, Stephen S., 4:53
Wistrich, Robert S., 8:38
Wohlfarth, Doris, Helen, and Siegfried, 4:31, 57; 5:50–51, 53–54, 57
Wolf, Captain, 2:69
Wolf, Shoshana, 6:71
Wolfe, Thomas, 2:37
Wolman, Ruth E., 8:35
Women of the Holocaust, 8:17, 22, 39

Jews are discovered hidden in a bunker during the Warsaw ghetto uprising, 1943.

World War I, *1*:**46**, 50–51;
　2:10–11; *3*:10–11
World War II
　allied invasion of Europe,
　　5:44–46, 63; *7*:67
　antisemitism after, *6*:22–23;
　　34
　beginning of, *3*:30
　ending of, *5*:72; *6*:9–11, 14 (map)
　pogroms after, *6*:22–23; *7*:72
Wyman, David S., *8*:8, 30

Y
Yad Vashem, *6*:52, 68, 70
Yahil, Leni, *8*:12, 27
Yellow star (of David), *3*:68–69;
　4:44, 62
Yiddish, *1*:39
Yochai, Boris, *5*:30
Yoors, Jan, *4*:63
Youth groups, Hitler, *2*:15, 24,
　30, 37, 65; *6*:9; *8*:36
Yugoslavia, *8*:8, 58

Women work at forced labor, Radom, Poland, circa 1940.

A memorial wall in the Education Center at the United States Holocaust Museum is made from 3,000 handpainted tiles created by American schoolchildren.

Z

Zionist movement, *1*:45; 6:34–43; 8:14

ZOB (Jewish Fighters Organization), *4*:40–41, 67–72

See also resistance groups

Zuckerman, Yitzhak, *4*:**41**; 8:24

Zweites Buch (Hitler), *7*:9

Zyklon B gas, *3*:43, 67–68

Photo Credits

Cover and Title Page: © Blackbirch Press, Inc.

Page 4: North Wind Picture Archives; page 5: Oesterreichische Gesellschaft fur Zeitgeschichte, courtesy of USHMM Photo Archives; pages 6, 26, 39: AP/Wide World Photos; pages 7, 31, 34, 49: Yad Vashem Photo Archives, courtesy of USHMM Photo Archives; pages 8, 23, 29: Bundesarchiv, courtesy of USHMM Photo Archives; page 9: Richard Freimark, courtesy of USHMM Photo Archives; page 11: David Wherry, courtesy of USHMM Photo Archives; pages 12, 19, 27, 36, 37, 45, 52, 59, 61: National Archives, courtesy of USHMM Photo Archives; page 13: Main Commission for the Investigation of Nazi War Crimes, courtesy of USHMM Photo Archives; page 14: KZ Gedenkstatte Dachau, courtesy of USHMM Photo Archives; pages 16, 37, 55: National Archives; page 17: Henryk Ross, YIVO Institute for Jewish Research, courtesy of USHMM Photo Archives; page 18, 63: courtesy of USHMM Photo Archives; page 20: American Jewish Archives, courtesy of USHMM Photo Archives; page 22: ©AFF/AFS Amsterdam the Netherlands; page 25: Gunther Schwarberg, courtesy of USHMM Photo Archives; page 32: Blackbirch Press Photo Archives; page 33: Aron Raboy, courtesy of USHMM Photo Archives; page 40: Joanne Schartow, courtesy of USHMM Photo Archives; page 42: Rijksinstituut voor Oorlogsdocumentatie, courtesy of USHMM Photo Archives; pages 44, 56: Archives of Mechanical Documentation, courtesy of USHMM Photo Archives; pages 47, 57, 58: YIVO Institute for Jewish Research, courtesy of USHMM Photo Archives; page 48: Frihedsmuseet, courtesy of USHMM Photo Archives; page 50: Prof. Leopold Pfeffenberg–Page, courtesy of USHMM Photo Archives; page 51: Jewish Historical Institute Warsaw, courtesy of USHMM Photo Archives; page 53: Rijksinstituut vor Oorlogsdocumentatie, courtesy of USHMM Photo Archives; page 54: Central State Archive of Film, Photo, and Phonographic Documents, courtesy of USHMM Photo Archives; page 60: on loan from the Wallenberg family to USHMM; page 62: Stadtarchiv Munchen, courtesy of USHMM Photo Archives.